Heterosexual
(A Love Song)

By

Chuck Taylor

Panther Creek Press

Spring, Texas

Published by Panther Creek Press
SAN 253-8520
116 Tree Crest
P.O. Box 130233
Panther Creek Station
Spring, Texas 77393-0233

Cover image from a photoengraving, "These Words Are All I Am," by
William Laufer, © 1997
Cover design by Adam Murphy
Houston, Texas

Manufactured in the United States of America
Printed and bound in Houston, Texas by
Houston Datum, Inc.

1 2 3 4 5 6 7 8 9 10

Library of Congress Cataloguing in Publication Data

Taylor, Charles (Chuck)

Heterosexual (A Love Song)

1. Poetry

2. Gender Studies

ISBN 0-977179753

Heterosexual
(A Love Song)

Table of Contents

There was a man, Walt Whitman, ... who began to define his own person, who began to tell his own secrets, who outlined his own body, and made an outline of his own mind, so other people could see it.

- Allen Ginsberg

Fever

In heterosexual love there's no solution. Men and women are irreconcilable, and it's the doomed attempt to do the impossible, repeated in each new affair, that lends heterosexual love its grandeur.

– Margerite Duras

For jazz singer Peggy Lee (1920-2002)

poet,

screenwriter,

author,

painter,

songwriter,

and humanitarian

I.

Welcome, friends and strangers, the subject is
Vance, he's above average in height, brown

eyes, skinny Ichabod Crane legs, big nose–
yet sweet face and broad shoulders; these words are

for strangers and friends, though most likely
few will make it all the way through; his friends

are hard working, lacking in idle time,
and they'd rather be living than reading

about life in a long report with the
butt ends of days that remain after the

gristle of labor, so welcome, strangers,
people I don't know, Vance sends welcome, through

me, the narrator, his love, who's a bit
too bubbly besotted, a thinker trained

to listen, possessing advanced degree in
bearing others' pains for cash. Poet Vance

imagines you, friends, as he dreams of strangers

who are young, who are old, who could be right

now living in an old Buick sleeping

on a side street in downtown Temple, in

the front seat, across from the Salvation

Army store; remember when Vance pulled in

next to you and your eyes met briefly, bro,

there were a couple of books along the

dashboard of your car – or maybe, stranger,

you are the woman crossing Anderson

Ave. in 1975, you are

pregnant, in a hippie Mexican kind

of embroidered dress and the sun is low

sending long golden orange lines of light up

the street to his eyes where Vance sits behind

the wheel of a 1957 truck

he bought for a hard-earned hundred, and the

wind caresses your dress, lifting it out,

and the sunlight shines through and suddenly

Vance sees you naked nude nothing under

that dress, in silhouette, crossing that street,

seven months pregnant he'd say, beautiful,

your bush hairs standing out, you might be that

woman, reader– how old's your child now, some

twenty-eight years old? and doing well, we hope,

stranger, friend of imagination, reader,

whose eyes could be kind and graceful; do scan

these lines, patient though unknowing where things

will go; right now we're headed to September

1964, we're in front of a

small town red brick church with your typical

modest Protestant steeple, and Vance is

11

wondering will he have friends show up for

this event, does he have friends, look at all

the people on her side, he thinks this means

he will not be old dying alone, he's

worried about a sad lonely death since

at four his parents left him alone to

sleep in a crib out on the "sun porch" where

in winter he'd get blue with cold, and he'd

shiver out before dawn *Can I get up?*

and his parents, irritated, tired,

would shout *No, go back to sleep!* and that may

be where his dislike of being told what

to do began, Vance really hates, always

will, and he doesn't like telling others

what to do either, altho' he's had to

do it and he knows plenty of folks – his

second, for instance – who loved ordering
others around (though her kids don't listen

anymore), but we're at a church wedding
in September 1964, and

he's happy someone will have him, he's drugged
on tranquilizers provided by Dad,

the doctor; the reverent Methodist
McCorkle, kindly and shyly smiles, but

Vance doesn't recall aisle marching to say
I do or what was sung, though he knows a

friend of the bride's from Spanish class sang from
the balcony for free; his wife-to-be's dad

lacked money for the wedding so Vance gave
a little and his father gave a lot,

Vance does recall at the Country Wheel Lodge
trying to cut the wedding cake and OOPS!

almost stabbing his bride in the neck, and

he recalls the wreak of a full week on

honeymoon with hardly no sex, troubled,

wondering well wasn't that why he got hitched?–

so they could simmer in erotic sheets

whenever they dreamed, but the wife, the new

wife, she threw herself later into pots

and pans, that was what she deemed the contract

of marriage, but at least they agreed on

one thing, they'd talked it over and over

before hitching, she and Vance agreed – *no,*

no kids, we're not going to have children,

no, not ever, because they did not like

the duty weight of children (though he had

little against children themselves), kids bored

you down, and she and he wanted to lead

adventurous lives, they did not want to
be grunting all the time to support kids,

stuck in the service sector at close to
minimum wage, she practical nursing,

he a hospital janitor, as they'd
done for many years when single. They had

a vision: they were going to live in
San Francisco, she'd get a part-time job,

he'd get a part-time job, and since they had
no kids, they'd have free time to go to rock

and roll shows, poetry readings, around
the town, art galleries, hang with other

writers and artists, maybe act in plays;
save up cash, quit work, travel to Paris

or Calcutta or Machu Picchu; *seize*
the day! carpe diem! you only come once

by this way so gusto at the grab, and

the sex was bound to get better as they

practiced, grew as one – these were thoughts around

and after the time of marriage during

time of Cold War, bomb shelter in his

grandpa's backyard, ICBM's erect

at our cities, at their cities; we're in

meltdown, thermonuclear brinkmanship,

Cuban missile threat 1962,

family friends throwing kids in their cars

and racing off to Canada north woods,

On the Beach showing the last surviving

American, in Australia, a sub

commander, waiting the arrival of the

radioactive dust cloud that ends all

mammal life on Earth; who wants kids

in such a bleak polluted providence–
how think long term? The government brain, it

seems, gets turned on only by booming dreams
of mushroom cloud music, plus his wife's dad

is furious at Vance for taking his
daughter to live in the oldest building

in Chicago, the coal furnace just on
the other side of a temporary

wall, pipes running zigzag on the ceiling,
but Vance thought the apartment suitable

non-bourgeoisie Bohemian, and she was
working now, he was trying to finish school,

studying it seemed all of the time, but
dreaming now of getting a Ph.D. for

good pay part-time teaching in San Fran, the
great lives they will lead, childless; his mother,

his father, groaning all his childhood years,
oh the weight we have struggled to carry, for

you, for sister, and *I never wanted*
children, his mother telling them, slamming

the door, locked on the sun porch, his sister
and he in front of the Howdy Doody

television, waiting for Daddy to
come home from his commute from the downtown

hospital Chicago, Vance always the
smallest boy when they lined 'em up in class

for photographs, small boy with buck teeth and
recessed chin; he gets kicked off the baseball

team in sixth grade, kicked out of the choir in
seventh, plays with outsider boys, his mom

shouts *Don't you dare let those jerks in our house!*
or even in the backyard after school,

except for Mark, the Jewish kid, except
for his friend the blimp, fat boy Larry, Vance

the outsider, his friends misfits too but
when high school came he couldn't even fit

with the boys in the leather jackets and
swept back Elvis hair, he did one play, got

on the track team, the magic club, the science
club, but never did much with any of

them, just remembers, at sixteen, sitting
in the basement of the suburban house,

alone, in love with Annette of full breasts,
brown eyes on Disneyland TV, then one

day, climbing up on that old love seat in
front of the television, climbing up,

pushing back the extra insulating his
father had tacked up to keep the sound of

the TV from polluting the living
room upstairs, and writing his name, the date

and time, his age, wondering out loud where
life will take, and promising some day to

return to look; and now his son, last night,
in Dallas, 2004, pacing the

floor at his girlfriend's house, his son Leo,
thirty-six, pacing around the table

where they have devoured take-out Chinese,
saying he had a traumatic childhood,

saying that Vance had abandoned him when
he was six, suddenly (true, when looking

at it from his point of view), though at the
time Vance thought he was leaving his wife

and the kids would remain in town for him
to love – so, now along with strangers and

neighbors I hope, Vance's two sons also the
audience, *his sons,* who never read books

of stories or poems, in this I hope they
will find relief and a reconciling.

II.

Switch scene, now it's 1968, King,
Martin, is assassinated, and then

Kennedy, Robert – brother of John,
the killed Kennedy president – is killed too,

the president in a limousine in
Dallas by the Texas Book Depository,

his brother, the Attorney General,
walking through a kitchen of a hotel,

and King, shot behind the Motel Loraine
in Memphis, Tennessee, by James Earl Ray;

Nixon wins the White House and we're all in
a state of shock, exhaustion, black and lost

beyond reconciling. Two high school friends,
Danny who ran with him on the track team,

and Ricardo, who taught him magic tricks,
are dead in Vietnam, both stepping on

mines during patrol. Vance has been going
to protests, standing on corners praying,

but now he is home, late evening, he's
is lying in bed waiting for his wife

to come out of the bathroom, hoping for
a slow ride to the stars, they're still living

in one of those run-down apartments, they
work as managers, an old big place filled

with students; she swishes briskly out of
the bathroom, his wife, and lets a strange phrase

slip from her mouth, he can't remember just
exactly what it was, something like, *I*

don't do the pill now and then, we might have
kids, a smirk on her face, a look he can

never forget, he leaps out of bed, *we're*
not having sex tonight, he says, *we're not*

having sex for a month. He mounts, in the
morning, a useless note on the bathroom

mirror, Please! Don't forget to take your pill!
A lot of good it does, in six months she's

rounding and he's mad, throwing fake punches
at her stomach, buzzing off in the car

for downtown Chicago each chance he gets,
obliviating her and it, thinking,

as he drives to the city, of her father
who dislikes him (maybe wisely and right),

pondering how he hides his bottles in
the basement and the garage; sometimes when

visiting Vance will catch a moment's glint
from above a vent or under a work

bench, those gin bottles, vodka and bourbon
bottles, the small ones that seem designed to

slip inside the breast pocket of a suit,
he's thinking of Norwegian Bob from Butte,

Montana, his father-in-law, the car
salesman, his long drunken rambles during

visits of Christmas season football games,
bitter angry rumblings taxing his dreams,

such lost desires, *I could have made it, I got
in on the ground floor, right after the war,*

*when General Motors was taking off –
the Automobile Age! – I could have made it*

big in the company, but the kids kept
coming, you know, every year, one more

mouth to feed and I couldn't take risks; oh
you know I love them all, all six of them,

I loved them but I couldn't travel as
GM wanted, I had to get a job

near home, to help Sharon out, I couldn't
leave her to all that work at home, no, me

gone the weekends too, and her by herself
in that lonely house in the country, no,

I had to squash my dreams, I had to give
them up, but look at these kids, wonderful —

aren't they? — and you're lucky to be picked
by the one who's most like her mother, so,

ah, I don't quite get what you're doing, Vance,
this school stuff, making your wife work, what are

you up to? cause it doesn't seem right to
me, you're a man now and got a degree,

you need to get a job and raise some kids –
yeah, Vance almost said, be miserable,

bitter and drunk like you, like you, Bob, bald
man who complained always how his teeth hurt

but wouldn't go to the dentist; Vance sees you
now (though you're long dead, in a heart attack

running across a restaurant parking
lot in the rain) – he sees you now in a

chair being fussed over by your daughters
Eve, Jane and Pat – they are giving you a

shampoo and permanent, they are scrubbing
your bald head and the hair around back and

around the ears, and Vance took it then (though
it might not now seem that way), as a sign

of your impotence, your enslavement to
the womb, *Now don't move Dad, sit still, you can't*

get up, we've got to fix your curly thick
red hair, and you're rolling your eyes in mock

anger and pure pleasure, your tongue stuck in
your cheek, and Vance thinking this man is a

broke back mule, he has no life of his own,
he's been enslaved by sexual drive

and by his wife's desire to procreate,
this man wants me to kill our life as he's

killed his, that's what he's thinking as he sees
the bald head shampooed; sex is a cruel jest

of God, an evil thing, the original
sin as Augustine of Hippo said (who

Vance was just then reading); sex is the fall
from grace, from the garden where once the lion

and the lamb lay down together, into
the toil of soil, the thorn of roses and

the blood and pain of baby birthing; sex,
passed from Eve and Adam, worm slithering

dumb into our operating systems
at around twelve or so, starts maddening

dreams, hijacks souls and bodies, and makes us
do what God in nature wants – populate

the Earth to choking; forget ideal dreams,
hopes to make exceptional life, to make

a better world. Yearn instead for naked
skin, for bare ass; the virus has grabbed our souls;

things were fine until the full consuming
itch between the legs – so here's the track all

laid down for men, you can date awhile, you
pick a girl to focus on and court, you

get engaged, married, get a job, then slave
to keep the lady pleased in her baby

making machine, yes you may do college,
both learn a career perhaps, but your job

is the big main thing while her focus is to
be in the home, popping them babies out

and raising kids. How does that sound – great – huh? –
heaven? – what god intended? Vance used to

walk the streets with his blimp friend Larry, tell
him the Queen Ants rule, forget about all

the male presidents and senators, the
Queen Ants rule, and we're the drones, we exist

to feed the Queen who is center of the
hive, we are nothing but drones, the way he

looked at his weary father in his long
commute to work in downtown Chicago,

the way he saw the sadness in Larry's
dad's eyes, back and forth, back and forth, in the

monoxide, and what for, he saw each day
in the sullen sadness of men's eyes, Vance

heard in the alcoholic rages voiced at
the evening table and in his sleep.

I *hate my job, I hate my job, I hate*
my job, if it weren't for the children I

wouldn't be trapped in this grind I hate...but ah,
then for Vance, then, as a boy, hope came, down

at the dim smoke shop along the railroad
commuter tracks, hope in pictorial

form, hid behind, a furtive thing, a
magazine that if they see you reading

they'd boot you from the store, no, they would not
sell to you, underage, not eighteen, but

you got hold of copies somehow, found guys
older to buy or found stores that would break

the rules and sell, you got and kept them hid
in secret places in your rooms, reading

them with flashlights under blankets till just
before dawn, the gnosis, secret sacred

knowledge, the *Playboys*, the *Dudes, Nuggets, Gents,*
the naked ladies, the lovely buxom

naked ladies and never the babies,
never children pictured running around

these nude women, and then, Holy Yahweh,
Faustian bargain, the final frontier

conquered, salvation, defeat of nature
by technology, the womb controlled, we

ruled, man *were we boss!* – first houses central
heat, then air conditioning, cars and planes

to defeat distances and time, and drugs
to defeat diseases, but now, now, the

pill, the pill, the pill – sing Hallelujah,
sing miracle, joy to the world, the truth

is come, God's benevolent and we've been
blessed! – there could be life now, he could love

a woman, the knives of cunt were blunted,
Poe's maelstrom calmed, gone the "appalling voice,

half shriek, half roar, a terrible funnel,"
no more the pit, the sinkhole, the suck hole,

no more the mouth with fangs, the tender trap;
the dark void's filled with flowers, and the rose

of passion, the pleasure that D.H. wrote
in *Lady Chatterley's Lover* (kept hid

in his parents' bookshelf), that pleasure could
be ours and we could love, sex to sex and

heart to heart and mind to mind because we

could choose, no longer bound to the meat wheel

of nature, God's omnipotent demand

of life nailed down to a sacrificial

cross of reproduction, the state taking

a small step *back* from heavy oppression

of joy when they made birth control against

the law. Any adult now, with a script

from the doc, can get the pill. So, reader,

you ask, how does one handle Vance's view of

women? How do I, the therapist, put

up with *sinkhole* or *suck hole* as names for

tender parts? How do I handle such terms?

Let's be frank. Fear of the female other –

cruel misogyny – whatever you want

to call it – will always live in men, as

lives in women fear of men, and we've got
good reasons to fear each other as this

report lays out. Fears are natural, or
as the philosophers say, existential,

built into our existence together,
to be transcended, one hopes, by the work

of love – bi and gay couples, they have their
own tensions to transcend by love's learned

trade – but I do digress, drift off subject –
Vance feels saved by the new techno device,

the pill. The tangle of sex is erased;
good bye to Norwegian Bob, hiding booze

in basement and garage, good-bye to Vance
mom howling, never wanting kids, breaking

plates against the kitchen wall, good-bye
to father's shouting drunken curses at the

dinner table, good-bye and hello love
and freedom, hello pleasure and freedom,

hello control of destiny, *we woke*
up one morning and our lives were set on

freedom, oh we woke up one morning and
our lives were set on freedom, and if Vance

can court a girl, a nonconformist, smart girl
somewhere who can think and want to get off

the meat wheel of reproduction, a girl
who didn't want to make her man into a

swayback mule, who didn't wish to claim to be
a Queen Ant fixed inside her hormones at

the center of the hive, a woman who
dreamed of travel and sights, of Marrakech and

Istanbul and Paris, Rio and
Vancouver, Kyoto and Peking – Vance

could, if he set myself to a diligent
search, find a woman who wanted to step off the

meat wheel, Yes? No? He knew his soul, he knew
his limits, not made by God to labor

forty hours a week in some downtown spot
till sore and old and farty, why he'd worked

since he was twelve, delivering papers,
riding his bike on slick iced suburban

Chicago streets, he'd mowed lawns and cleaned as
janitor an insurance office, yes,

rising at five to fold the newspapers,
cutting lawns on Saturdays, cleaning the

office on Sundays, he knew the world of
work; he'd done it, he'd had enough; he liked

to hike in woods, he liked long Russian novels,
liked pool downtown in the dusky pool hall

next to the smoker's shop, he despised the
forty hour work week, selling his soul in

large slices of day for pay when this was
a postwar world awash in wealth and trash,

no more a need for depression values
based on a scarcity culture at this

consumer time, no, and Vance knew he was
not stable enough to sweat that way, he

knew with his torn, now divorced parents,
that his anger would bust out in a flood

of drink like his dad. Yet many years
Vance stuck in towns he despised, in work he

despised that stressed to the edge of break
his soul; one lost night drinking he took off

in his car to never come back, got as
far as Tucson when the dollars ran out,

calling from an old motel for money

to be telegraphed to return him home,

another night drunk in San Antonio,

on the river walk, he tries to get a

waitress to run away to Mexico.

His mother, who never worked, oddly was

a kind of model, his ma who never

left the house and had no friends,

and his grandfather, who retired at fifty,

who read and kept a journal and joked and

laughed at the pleasure of life, he was his

model, grandfather James; and yes, Vance knew

limits, it wasn't he despised the cute

ball routines of babies loud screaming and

shitting, keeping you up half the night – no,

not that, nor the child who refused to go to

bed or take a nap, no, that's not what got

to him; kids are cute, they're your alternate

reality, they keep the kid in a

guy alive, he loves to play with kids, he

finds himself at parties bored with adults,

he finds the upstairs room where children are

playing and he drops from responsible

skin to the floor where they play, they laugh and

goof, with plastic trucks and teddy bears, Vance

might do a few coin or rope tricks (he made

his living once doing children's magic) –

yes he loves to be with kids, and it's no

wonder his sons called him *Vance*, not the

respectful *Dad*, because he could be a

kid easily with them; they'd quickly mop

and glow part of the wide kitchen floor and

then in socks dash across the dining room
carpet and go sliding, sliding, the boys

and he, across the kitchen floor, he'd tell
them of the toilet frog that could suck them

down (getting out his frustration blues) or
of the dark bowlers in the skies who made

thunder and lightning, ah he could play, he
didn't like parenting much, but he sure

could get into play, *Vance, Vance*, not *Dad*, not
the male-disciplined toiler who mules

home the bacon, responsible guy, who
cuts the edges and trims the grass, no, not

your Mister Sacrificer, t'was not in
the cards, t'was not the dream he'd made of man-

woman love looking at the nudie mags
of his youth, reading Hugh Hefner's "Playboy

Philosophy." He knew he'd never have
the wealth to own a mansion, to love like

Hef the buxom beauties on rotation
every six months, but Vance hoped to be

lovable enough perhaps (he didn't know,
pimpled and adolescent) to find one,

in the wide field of maidens, who shared his
odd view of life – and he did, she said yes,

those Chicago nights they dated for two
years late talking in the Old Town folk clubs

close to the old Biograph theatre
where Dillinger was gunned down by G-Men,

betrayed by the lovely lady in red;
she agreed, she gave him her word over

and over, her word of honor that her
dreams of a free, childless couple life were

exactly the same, and then she betrayed,

the great fact never mentioned when talking

of the high number of divorces and

the disappearing fathers, how many

wives did betray, how many young men wanted

love but did not want the family ties,

how many lied to, how many tricked, that's

what's never told, the statistics never compiled,

no questioning the dictatorship of womb,

the right of women to decide without

bothering to consult their mates; in his

own small circle Vance could point to numbers

of cases, women who admit doing

it to their men, and men who seethe as Vance

once seethed, and Vance can tell you of his

own second son Paul, wed to Winifred

six years, suspicious from the start, growing
more suspicious, demanding finally

a paternity test, the girl proved not
his, the horrid blow done to Paul and to

their family love and to Tasha not
his who he must by law, till grown, support,

and it's not, dare we say, dearly
imagined reader, purely a male deal,

you may have seen the movie *The Hours*, I've
told you of Vance's mom, shouting, shattering

dishes, *I never wanted kids,* but in the
movie, the mother of the poet, the

mother of the poet dying of AIDS
(she's made a MONSTER in his novel and

poems), she shows up after his suicide,
after he's jumped out the window, she comes

to the funeral, much older of course,
more at peace than she appeared earlier

in the film, having worked a life as a
librarian, she returns, this woman

who earlier in the film was so sad
and miserable, despite the loving,

struggling efforts of her husband, so sad
that she drops her son off at a sitter

and goes, pregnant with second child, to a
smart hotel to kill herself, this woman

in the film, a solitary soul, made
miserable by middle class post World

War II suburban comfort, so she's cruel
to her son and wants to kill herself, setting

her prescription pills out on the hotel
bed, lying down, weeping, and yet, she doesn't –

she walked away from family instead,
after the birth of the second child, left

the man and made a life of her own, in
the movie, *The Hours*, based in part on the

life of Virginia Woolf and on the
influence of her books, so it's not just

men, not just one of the genders in this
heterosexual prison dance, Woolf

couldn't take the smothering suburban life,
the heterosexual monotonous

monogamy of it – I doubt that he,
Vance, ever grasped the size of the mountain

he pushed against, that dominating myth
of our time, celebrated in almost

every Hollywood movie, the one
true way, the only acceptable line,

marriage and family, *I am looking*
for a man I love so much I want him

as the father of my children, Vance's
students write in their poems for class. The one

doctrine, the only path for many – more
female, some men – that makes their present pain

worth suffering. They never watch the news,
they're not involved in politics, to

hover after work in the womb of love
in family – that's all that makes sense to

most of the young these days, and Vance, when young,
did not reject the doctrine whole, he wanted

life like those great turn of the century
activist-journalist-poet writers,

like Louise Bryant and John Reed, a hot
adventurous family of two, man

and wife, Bohemian, off to cover
Poncho Villa in the revolution

of Mexico, off to Russia to see
the Bolsheviks seize power in Moscow,

but foolish dreamer Vance, he was betrayed,
she said she was using the pill – not that

Vance had ever much sex married to your
mother, he says politely to you, his

sons, fearing to hurt – and you, strangers,
friends, I hope you dig this soulful honest

candor in our time of lip-zip lying
hypocrisy, and Vance, I say, says thanks to

all who've come this far on our crooked crank
of a journey, no abstract bullshit spun

here and I know Vance is oddly glad. *He
was betrayed but he chose life, friends.* You know

his second son doesn't call and Vance has
not seen Paul in thirteen years. It pains Vance

deeply, I know – I'm the third wife, his best
friend – pains Vance to see his sons struggle in

pain, to watch their divorces like his splits,
their trying to love their kids who came when

they were not ready, as Vance tried, in a
less successful way, to love you and your

brother, to not pass on to you the curse
(though it seems he did), because he knew of

course the mother's betrayal wasn't your fault.
I've run out of words, sons, friends, strangers,

I can only turn to what I saw on
TV's *Montel* last Wednesday, before noon

while munching a sandwich between clients
in a small room off my office, the show

shows a Caroline being interviewed
by Montel about how she went to look

at new baby clothes at a friend from work's
apartment, then when the friend had her in

the door, she shot Caroline, split her open
with a kitchen knife, jerked out her baby,

then drove to the nearest hospital, to
claim that the six month fetus she had in

a plastic sack was her own, that *she* had
accidentally aborted; the woman

had been telling her family that she was
pregnant and the family had just held for

her a baby shower, and here, on the
show *Montel,* they're talking to Caroline

who survived amazingly, and to Carl,
her husband; it's extreme you say, and I

agree, of course – extreme, but the margins
illuminate the center, I'd say – but

Vance, he often sees the lady in his
dreams, the Mexican dress gal slow crossing

Anderson Ave, yes (it almost makes
me jealous telling this), and the sun low

on the horizon in long orange-ish streaks
lighting up her walk, her dress billowing

out and the sun of conception in the
breeze displaying in glory her glory

of breast and cunt and child filled mound; it's such
a comic cosmic act, and Vance is old,

now in grandpa phase, brain cells altered,
heart remade – only *I,* his wiser half,

his former therapist who, against all
rules, fell in love with the man she treated,

dare take him back to his early ego's
whine. Only I can ask, *Vance, was that you?*

Were you so poor in heart? Could you be that
sad man pictured earlier sleeping in

the car near the Salvation Army with
paperbacks strewn across a dusty dash?

We therapists have a trick we use on
patients; it seems that whatever they latch

onto, whatever dreams, conscious or
unconscious, they bring up in therapy,

these dreams are bright keys unlocking suppressed
selves, secretly speaking back to their selves.

Do I sound too technical? If you dream
of a washing machine, you're the machine.

Got it? A lost part of yourself calls from
your dream in the mask of the machine –

but I digress again, I'm new at this
poet's writing game, counting syllables

by ten, stanzas by two – no long song here
to save the world today before you all learn

to redeem yourselves – but back to the man
patient who became my man. Vance doesn't

buy my theories all the time, that he's
the man sleeping near Salvation Army.

His snort makes me laugh, but I don't forget –
though you may call me besotted with love,

incapable of objectivity –
the pain was real for sons and former wives,

the pain is still alive in their faces,
deep hurt, though they have made other loves; yes

besotted like I, though we are perhaps
too old to be besotted, too many

times in love, too often a part of the
slow decline of love, the fading away

of years worn in a slow painful habit
turned narcotic, nightmarish, where you feel

there can be no resurrection, but besotted, I'll
call me besotted, at this time, these two

years, a learning and forgetting, us two,
out of other heterosexual

lives; I, a mother of three now grown, a
woman who wanted children and can't see

not wanting children; what Vance, my husband,
calls the meat wheel I call the wheel of life,

we are farmers here in love's learned trade
of plowing and planting, harvest and care,

from generation to generation,
parent to child or patient – yet at times

I wonder if regeneration can
come to all good hearts here or ever,

take his younger son Paul, all his troubles,
the running away from home and living

on the street and then in the crack house, thrown
in juvenile detention center, thrown in

the county jail later for months so when
Vance came to visit he had to peer through

bullet proof glass and converse by phone, twice
in drug treatment centers, years in AA,

at age twelve pulling a knife on Vance and
stabbing him in the leg; Vance lies sleepless

in guilt night after night, grovels, curses,
cries for the crooked way things turned, for what

his son, beautiful Paulie, so gentle,
so sensitive as a small child, has been

through, but then Vance will turn in bed, sit up,
flip on a light and scratch out a poem, and

tell himself, hey, the boy's now thirty-five,
he gets to blame his problems on his dad

just until he's twenty-five – then he's on
his own; he chose his fate more than I, and

now he lives it, gets to play the long truck
drives and pleasures of the crack pipe, short times

home with wife and kids. I guess Paul and I,
we're divorced; I can say bye-bye, Paulie,

bye-bye, prodigal son, Ishmael kid –
no more the stealing and the lies, though I

hold still a dream of regeneration,
to walk half way to meet and embrace your

voice amongst the good music that swells in
the charged atmosphere of what we love;

and Vance, he chose his fate too, one lived and
loved in a rough Bohemian manner,

not in San Fran, but in Tejas, near his
sons, and Vance is not a bitter father,

he has his memories, like riding in
his hundred dollar Ford down the alley

behind Bluebonnet Plaza onto Rice
Road near the Long John Silver's fish place, so

full of life, so careless about his death
or the deaths of his children, no seat belts

then, bouncing through potholes; he'd pulled off at
the Firestone to get a gas cap to take

the place of cap he'd lost, this during the
oil crises of '73, he so

happy *not* to be working, to have quit his
regular job to househusband at home

with his kids in the ugly tract house north
of the airport, taking the boys hiking

in the remnant of woods that survived
just beyond the airport fence, finding a

small stream, full of rusted cans and plastic
bags, but pretending to fish, that they were

really fishing, in the little quarter
of nature left somewhat undisturbed,

unbulldozed, he means, by the city, the
lovely looks on his boys' faces, how he loved

them then, how for the moment he felt free
and did not feel betrayed or enslaved to

a life not his choosing, and then, was it
in 1978 when he got a house

in that small town that came with an acre? –
keeping ducks and chickens and goats, growing

corn and beans and the yellow meated kind
of watermelon, all organic, no

pesticides, no fertilizers of a
chemical kind, the corn side packed with cow

manure that neighbor Philip gave them,
canning in glass Ball jars from the orchard,

apples and peaches, getting water to
drink from a spring, gathering along the side

of highway fallen branches to burn in
the fireplace for cooking and heat, the kids

griping at first, then growing to love it,
the family closeness that comes from labors

shared away from life as crazed consumption –
ah at night, in the ancient moon glow they'd

stroll country roads twisting through silvered live
oaks, Vance in his second marriage then, a

new life more to his choosing with three more
kids to care for but much better loving,

though another drinking father-in-law,
military Colonel, racist, angry,

retired and lazy, broiling all day
in front of the television, red faced

at commies everywhere, no better than
the bitter first father-in-law, now seen

as a kind man really, a good man, though
he'd drunk a life away in pain of loss.

III.

I suppose it's time to provide a scene
romantic, sexy. Vance wanted this report

in verse to be dedicated to his
hero after all, the cocksman romance

male novelist, Henry Miller, almost
drowned many times himself in the frenzied

heterosexual majestic swirl
of the maelstrom – you put your penis in

her cunt, and the small boat of your life goes
"speeding dizzily round and round with

a swaying sweltering motion" (says Poe
as quoted by Vance). Your swirling, whirling

selves lost in the sucking maelstrom of life.
Yet Vance was never a player chasing

seductions one after another in
the speed of dazing days, trying to bag

in bed candle lighted chick after chick,
sexy music playing; no, he stuck like

fly paper to his few buzzing passions,
his wives and two long term lovers, and so

no screaming rages here, sorry, nothing
thrilling to spice up, no violent reds,

no one gets punched or slashed; Vance does demur
when I ask about his other loves, he

doesn't try to change the subject, just stops
speaking, in respect, he says, for a passion

moment's dignity. Those she's are gone from
his present wave, he says, yet in the time

capsule of memory he doesn't judge,
he doesn't remake history loveful

or hateful; in the times now gone the she's
still care and he still cares, he'll say. Vance does

admit that what in memory remains
are not the anniversaries, are not

the births, are not the birthdays or tender
words, but passion, the burning fevered blood

fertilizing the soul. Mainly, he says,
a bit sheepishly, he recalls doing it,

on mountain tops, in rivers and bushes,
in elevators, on hiking trails, in trees,

at the park, upstairs at parties, in the
backyards of neighbors, the kitchen table,

but mostly slow afternoons in their beds
in the long spaces of his poetic

daze, the main problem for your teller now,
being, how does one keep up with this? In

life that's not so hard and always fun – on
boats, the hot tub, we do – but on paper?

Should sex be presented from my point of
view or from Vance's point of view? From the

man's we'd see breasts rise as her spine straightens
and her back arches, or perhaps we'd see

a tender shoulder; from the woman's, what?
It could be arms, even the skinny shape

of legs, or hang of balls – anything that
lights the heart and spins through the circuits of

of love to sex. What does it matter, when
we have love, when we're going to flow, you

and all, into dinosaur extinction
(though probably not as well marked in rock

or sediment), when our sun will die and
our green and friendly Earth will grow as cold

as an asteroid in the far void. Does
it matter? What matters? The bees down to

the flower pollen, the rutting antler
dance of the caribou, the ying, the yang,

still searching out the strange other in some
far bright planet outer space? I'm seeing

my aunt, seeing her now asleep upstairs
in the old big house where she raised three sons;

the alarm beeps, it's seven and her blue
eyes, as blue as ever, flicker open.

She thanks the Lord for another day, she's
seventy-nine and in a grieving group

with other widows at the church, her husband
Bill, eighty-two, died six months ago, oh

I loved them, knew all my life! – still see my
aunt sitting in the kitchen, breast feeding

my cousin after he was a born, I
there "helping" at five, was it? – she and Bill

were married for fifty years...and why do
I write around the sheets of such subjects,

why the maelstrom heterosexual?
How about war? Isn't that always the

way, micro or macro, where the king comes
up on horse with his knights, we're the peasants

in the black soil digging for potatoes,
and the king says the country's endangered,

ignorant armies gather at borders,
so rise up from your fields of labor to

save our nation – isn't that where long poems
lie? Love and war, war and love, Helen and

Paris, Ulysses and Penelope? Don't
ask me – I'm just a therapist making

a poetic report on a poet –
but does anyone bore through epics now

except in required college classes?
Ah here I've done it again, slipped the noose

of narrative, my thoughts like a pinball
bouncing around, setting off zingers and

lights; the longer the silver ball takes to
reach the hole, its destination, the more

the points light up, the more you win; work those
flippers, you pin ball wizards, shake that box,

keep that ball jumping and jingling, and bless
all digression – to those who say I use

a metaphor that's male, I say, remake
the metaphor! – those balls are ovaries,

happy, dancing in fields, not sitting, not
waiting. I should take a break now, fix a

meal, watch a little *Oprah*, take a nap,
but I'm troubled, thinking of refugees

in Chad from the Sudan, drawing dirty
water from a quickly dug well, their mules

dying around them, the men disappeared
into the Sudanese civil war, the

children malnourished, facing starvation

when the rains come bringing floods in the sparse

desert, TV shows them, and Vance's pleas, his

common family pains, seem a petty light,

silly, like Haley's comet last time 'round.

Still, Vance's grown a good life from wrecked soil –

a life to meet with open eyes the end.

Yes he claims a life: he left his children,

he left them, to go chasing metaphors,

so poor he had no cash for rent, later

the lonely poet staying on the beach

in Galveston in an old truck amongst

seagulls and sunrises – he believed in poor

living ideally because of being raised

well-to-do if not rich, and yearned for the

holy travail of great travel, a bush

hippie dedicated to the true Light
of the Poem, living a year in a tent

in the woods above Sanchez Creek, Dallas,
Texas, the year of 1987 –

performing poems on bright buses, dim bars;
publishing books of poems by his buddies,

sleeping six months in the basement of a
used bookstore on the floor by the sump pump

in a room where bugs – water beetles and
cockroaches mostly – crawled all over his

body, but ah! the books to read and the
poetry events they staged, the music,

the art shows, transcendent the earth of art
they dwelled in, and he survived at times as

a Kelly Temp at One Main Building in
downtown Dallas, typing for a firm in

architecture long specifications,

also folding letters and envelope

stuffing for a quick print shop, and once in

a rubber manufacturing plant – foam

rubber, that is – for sofa pillows and

mattresses, large chunks of it piled in

mountains they'd bounce off shoulders from one end

of the huge warehouse to the other. But

why, I as therapist, wish to ask – no

use of rubbers for birth control? Just one

could have changed your fate. Vance agrees, but

says they're torture, penis strangulation –

try kissing me with a nylon stocking

over your head – that'll give you a feel

for what those tiny torture tubes are like,

and the times, consider the times too; we

were taught, back in the sixties, a couple
of eggs were simpler to thwart with a pill

or with a diaphragm, than millions and
millions of wiggly, slippery male sperm –

so argued the audacious Germaine Greer,
feminist crazy for men, in her books.

Poet Vance believes that Milton had it
wrong, that therapists like me exist to

justify one man's ways to God. So my
work becomes rationalization? Well,

maybe that's as noble as work to stuff
a round peg into a square hole – that is,

to trim a person down into what is
labeled "normal" at the moment. Here is

one man's maelstrom wrestling to stand for
all the silences, for all men's stories

buried in unmarked graves so deep they go
untold, forgotten, except for a chip

of bone perhaps in the back of our brains
dim-calling, dim-pressing, out of the soil

of the gender, but now friends, sons, strangers,
can you begin to sense one ghost-haunted

man seeking out a path of redemption?
Vance flew to Chicago, knocked on the door

of his childhood house, pulled back down in the
basement the dusty insulation where

once was the TV room, to answer his
penciled scribble still legible since he

left at eighteen, to mark on those beams just
who he is and where he's been, and now he's

ready to stand up to consequences –
our Earth still here, not bombed, no polar ice

caps melted in apocalyptic flood.
He stands bowed, not exactly proud, for ways

he made a place in the Earth we're bound to,
a world God or humans or nature made

(or made by all three in a kind of trine)
where all must find a way, construct some dream

or personal map – *I say*, not Vance, me –
the teller here (they call me *Zoe*) – from what

you never see coming, mostly do not
choose, and never ever quite imagine.

Right friends, strangers, sons dear – who've tripped this far
inside this pilgrimage, dwelled here

an hour with these paper leaves or leavings?
Friends, strangers – you agree or disagree?

And Vance, my sweet, though at times we argue
and disagree, I, the besotted mate

and therapist, must offer up a kind
of key. My dear, my Vance, try to prance a

more lighthearted dance, to enhance your chance
for love and romance, to stay on board with me

on the love train, the love train, for a long
and happy ride, we together on the

love train, heading for a destination
great, the love train, with our old baggage left

behind, thanks to great therapy (I say
with irony). Still, take note: in play

heterosexual, you can be sure
of plenty of grandeur drama, but there

ain't no cure. *Chicks are born to give FEVER,*
morning noon and night. Peggy Lee, hero,

to whom I dedicate this report – not
Miller (forgive me) – you need to listen to. When

I was a girl, through mates, kids, grandkids, tough

Peggy sang *FEVER, chicks are born to give*

you FEVER, oh what a lovely way to

learn, what   a   lovely   lovely   way   to   burn...

January-July, 2004

Martin Luther King Day

for James

The man's standing some fifteen feet from Cal
while Cal's pumping the tank, the man's standing
in torn shirt, jeans, under the canopy—

out of the hard rain, when the cashier in
the station opens the door and yells, *Get
out of here, Stop bothering customers!*—

and the man turns, shouts, *I'm not, I'm just here
waiting for a ride, that's all!* And the clerk
goes back inside and Cal continues to

pump gas, keeping the poor man in his side
vision as a Cadillac pulls up to
the pump in front of Cal and the man runs,

knocks on the Caddy window to ask for
change. Cal's thirteen blocks down from the corner
of Martin Luther King Drive and the road

out of town. Cal pays, and then heads out with
PBS selections playing from the
speeches of Doctor King, headed now down

Chicon past the Nation of Islam
Building, beggars stumbling drunk in the rain
on the street, young girls under eaves flashing

legs into the pouring dark so Cal must
slow down; his wife's asleep on his right, his
daughter is focused on her Gameboy

in the back; Cal starts dreaming dull office
moves for the next day, his soul a slave to
empire, his dreams, though sad, still made for light.

Veteran Joe

for Daryl

Joe wanted to do big things and he's in
bed one morning trying to recall what

they were, those American dreams that kept
him hungry and running until his mid-

forties, what were they, Joe never wanted
money, took good pleasure in living with

no car, carrying the grocery sacks
home, and at times the water condensed

around the cold gallon milk jug soaking
the bottom of the brown bag and the milk

would torpedo through onto the sidewalk
as he shuffled along back to his room

in the theater downtown in the basement
Joe shared with a grinning Scottish boy who

dressed in leather pants and safety pins in
his ears, punk style, and worked the lights in the

theater; no, the dream was not money
wealth and it was not power—no way!—but

maybe the spiritual power of the
powerless it was, Joe working in a

print shop on Congress folding letters and
sticking them in envelopes three days a

week, the rest of the time sitting at Pete's
Bagel Shop with onion soup and a bagel,

reading a newspaper someone left on
a chair; what was he up to when so full

of American dreams, what did the paper
say was happening that night down on sixth

street where the clubs are? It is April and
the college students will be parading

on the wide sidewalks in spring ritual,
the blaring sounds of different bands

washing out of clubs onto the street. Joe
walks to Sixth and Trinity, and starts to

hunt for his daughter, by now he's had some
beers, stood on a corner to hear a blind

saxophone player, setting five dollars
in his tip jar. The blind guy's a Vet like

Joe is from Vietnam, drafted early,
combat in sixty-six, he lives in the

woods out by Barton Creek; he begs with a
sign along the road during the day; a

month ago he was swiped by a dump truck
hauling bricks, broke three of his ribs, you can

tell by the way he clutches his side while
playing his sax, Joe also talked to Frank,

a sad old man with a great art car that's
got children's toys glued on bright painted roof

and fenders; he's a Korean Vet, an
old infantryman who crossed the thirty-eighth

and nearly lost his feet in the cold, in
the mountains just south of Tumen river;

Joe's daughter considers herself grown up—
an adult, she says, at sixteen, she's dropped

out of school, left her mother's small duplex
to stay down the street in a big old house

with Sandra, a friend from school, whose mother
is a heroin addict and drives trucks; Rose

has on a halter top, she is spinning
a red carnation around and around

on her index finger, but if you look
closely you can see a pin protruding

from the bottom of the stem, from which she
spins the carnation. *Hi dad,* daughter says,

you got a new girlfriend? Buy her at least
twelve carnations and I go home early!

Rose comes up and gives him a hug, *Sorry*
I didn't get to the library to

hear you read from your new book, May took me
to the lake, Derek's her new boyfriend, he's

thirty-two, he works at Maggie Mae's Pub,
the Irish place just up the street. Rose should

be leading a normal life, Joe thinks. He
led a normal life when he was her age,

she should be in school, he was in school, he
was a long time at study, but the kids,

all three of them, they look, they think what good
did all the college degrees, graduate

and undergraduate, do for him or

mom, always scraping by? Does Joe dream or

does Joe get by? Joe gets by, dreams of old

dreams, his lost love Alexis, she worked in an

office downtown, she's a secretary;

Joe met her in the romance section at

Congress Avenue Books, took her hand, he,

veteran, in the romance section, she

moved away, out of the B authors down

to the letter O (it said on the shelf),

Joe approached her, he took her hand again,

she giggled, shrugged her shoulders, they walked

over to the Bagel Shop and talked, she

wore no makeup, she said, because her child

was grown and now she felt so old she had

given up on men, she stopped dyeing her

hair, let all the gray show, and Joe said he
liked the gray, all the while wondering how

big was her house, did it have a big tub,
maybe they could do it in the shower,

how long would she let him stay at her place
before she'd get upset that he didn't

work, they always got upset at his lack
of drive, as if they were going to be

doing the child thing all over again,
these older women—if they needed to

nurture—why not take care of a
nice vet guy, Joe doesn't dream, just watches

the telly now (that's what the Brits call it),
Joe's never been to merry England, no,

not to the Sorbonne in Paris, France, not
to the Alhambra in majestic Spain,

never much of anywhere, outside of
Vietnam and short leaves to Tokyo,

a local boy raised in Killeen, his dad
at the base, a distant man, a sergeant,

his mother from Arkansas, a housewife,
worked part-time at Safeway, his mother still

alive, Joe takes the bus next day out to
see her, Joe cuts her grass, he replaces

a leaky hose on her washer; when Joe
walks streets of Killeen people stare at him,

they don't dig the tattoos on his arms and
they don't approve of his long gray beard,

he can't write here, his father's shoes are still
in the front closet, *Why don't you throw out*

the shoes, ma, dad's been dead five years. I will,
I will, she says, so Joe goes on the bus

back to downtown Austin to the playhouse,

for his reading—a story, a few poems,

in the building where in the basement Joe

lives, they've done the place up with darkness and

candles, no sets from any productions,

between shows, people sit on the floor, what

people there are at readings in this fan

music town, mostly the same Joe's seen at

other readings; his daughter's not there, Joe's

doing a story published last year in

a magazine from Dallas, a hundred dollars

on publication and a hundred bucks

now, not bad for a veteran living

in a room in a basement, a few poems

too (as he said), an old fashioned ballad

about a man who lost his wife to a

wrestler (true), not Joe, he lost his wife to
a computer programmer, another

poem about his daughter, his family and
how he misses them, how he remembers their

walks together on bright Sunday mornings
along town lake under the cypress trees.

Was it Joe dreamed of life as Popper said
in *Leisure as the Basis of Culture*,

was it Joe dreamed that corporations would
be owned not by the state but by the ones

who actually did the work, worker
owned General Electric etceteras, was

it he dreamed humankind would learn to
harbor the egalitarian spirit

of God in all things, was it Joe trusted
to the truths of American Whitman,

Resist much, Obey little—and what of
all these grieving years of glum filled wars,

his nation fighting in far away states
—Panama, Iraq, Nicaragua,

island Granada the size of Austin, what of
all these stupid wars, the dead, the wounded,

living in VA anger and despair?
All the outsider causes he'd espoused

in prose and verse since his discharge stateside.
Joe starts by reading a sonnet he wrote

in two hours over at Pete's bagel—
no question it needs more work—when someone

stands up in the dark of the audience,
a woman—who is it? She's just standing

there, or is she inching forward, Joe tries
to stare under the spotlight, to make out

her face, she's carrying something—what?—an
umbrella? She's now in the light of the

spot and Joe sees wide green eyes, a strong chin,
yes, it must be Alexis, the woman

he picked up in the romance section
of the bookstore, Joe lived with her out in

Tarrytown by MoPac for six months, a
nice house, small backyard with big trees, he wanted

to run a permanent garage sale out of
the place, but she wouldn't think of it, no,

though he called her the apple of his eye,
she called him sunflower, she called the cops

and had Joe removed from the house, what did
she want now, she's got a gun, she's going to

shoot him, no, it's a box, he left a box
of poems behind, no, she says she wants to

read, why can't I read, this event is paid
for by tax money, my money, I write

as good as you, I raised three kids, I kept
a house, I work, I pay taxes. You can't read,

Joe groans back at her, you weren't asked to read,
you hold, of this life, a sentimental

view, like Erma Bombeck, like Ann Landers;
this is art, it's not your turn, we gave up

all to deal in the sweet coin of words;
you see buddies blown up stepping on those

claymore mines in the paddies on patrol,
you see Kennedy, King, and Kennedy

again, assassinated, the best minds
of your generation destroyed by mad

men; *when you publish, get stories or poems*
printed in magazines, then you can read,

Joe says, and she's pushing as he speaks, she's
a big woman, but Joe is holding on,

what were those dreams, American dreams, he's
wondering, embarrassed by the drama,

what were the big things, what the grand changes
we dreamed so hard and certain were coming—

Joe's not small, he's not shoving, just holding
on, *when you've suffered loss like we've suffered...*

Kick The Can

for Chico

I really enjoyed kick the can, I don't
know why we don't kick the can anymore,
I enjoyed the sweat and the yelling in

the simmer of summer, I enjoyed bangs
on the shins and the falling down on the
concrete street, and the swearing and getting

up in the consummation of August,
yeah, and I enjoyed climbing trees too, I
enjoyed hugging the trunk with legs and arms

and skinnying up till you got to a
branch and then climbing higher and higher—
sometimes we'd have races up the trees, there

were rules about that, what you could do, cut
the guy off, blocking his way with a leg
so you got first to the top, but no blows

with a fist or kicking cause you didn't
want to knock a guy out of a tree, and
then at the top, you might bend this way and

that to make the tree swing like you were a
god, and I really enjoyed sneaking out
at night, climbing out the bedroom window

onto the roof of our family car,
then meeting some buddy at four AM,
say maybe where they were building a new

home. We'd have nothing to do, little to
say, but we felt triumphant, and I'd climb
back off the car's roof back inside, and my

dad, I don't know if he ever noticed
the foot marks, but he never said a thing,
he was young too, I guess, and I really

enjoyed exploring around in the trunks
up in the attic, opening boxes,
taking out all the old stuff, the World War

One and World War Two military stuff,

uniforms and medals and photos, the

old journals of my grandfather, the dress

form my mother never used anymore

since clothes were now bought ready-made at

the department store, and I'd stay up there

in the August dust and heat, stay up there

till my mother started shouting my name,

I'd let her shout till her voice worried a

little, and then I'd come down and feel loved;

they say I had a tough childhood, my ma

was a shut-in and had no friends, and my

dad was a drunk who often did not show

up till late at night, sometimes dumped at the

curb by a taxi, then mom would drag us

out of bed to help drag dad across the

lawn and up the front steps into his bed,

but mostly we were left alone, you know,

we weren't told what to do and weren't shut down

by stupid rules, so I loved my childhood,

at least till school started and we had to

sit in rows all day and be told what to

think. I'm sorry that kids don't have childhoods

like the kind we had; I'd like to finish

by quoting my favorite poet-sage from

China, from around 604 BC,

'When people lose sight of the way to live

came codes of love and honesty," Lao Tse.

Laws come when people lose the way, that god

of heart that teaches natural and free.

Windows

for Peggy Lynch

I've been asked to write a short poem about
windows, but the truth is I don't much like

windows, I much prefer doors; it seems glass
windows were more likable in the old

days when you could open them, when you could
climb out of them, say late at night when your

parents were sleeping; windows in the old
days were built closer to the floor, they slid up

and down easy on a counterweight, I
helped my dad repair one when I was in

sixth grade; now I am a modern old high
office tower man, yet back at my house,

the high school girl who lives across
the street has "I love Slade" soaped on her

bedroom window; each night I walk the dog
I check the glass to see if she still loves

Slade; one night a young man pulled up in front
of my house in a beat-up car and I

saw the girl climb out her window—not an
easy feat because it was a modern

window high off the ground. She got into
the beat-up car, presumably with Slade.

So maybe windows are useful after
all. Maybe they can serve as doors and your

soul can get beyond all that hard yearning,
into the dirt and flowers of the world.

Books by Chuck Taylor

Poetry:

The Breaking that Brings Us Anew (Folder Press, 1978)
Selected Poems (Goethe's Notes, 1978)
Always Clear and Simple (Aileron, 1981)
Ordinary Life (Cedar Rock, 1984)
Amerryka! (Ruddy Duck, 1984)
Drinking in a Dry County (Maelstrom, 1985).
I am Delighted that You are Here (Fat Tuesday, 1995)
Letter to the Lizard King (Press of Circumstance, 1995)
Poet in Jail (Pygmy Forest Press, 1997)
Flying: A Primer (Tsunami, 2004)
Rips (Unicorn, 2005)

Fiction:

Somebody to Love (Flatland, 1991.
It All Flows Away (Tsunami, 2004)

Essays:

Only a Poet (Cedar Rock Press, 1984)
Poet in Jail (Pygmy Forest, Albian, Ca. 1997)

Bio Moment

The author can't think of much to write that hasn't already been written in a different biographical moment.

From the Mormons, while living in Salt Lake City and serving as CETA poet-in-residence, the author borrowed the idea of a once a week family time, so every Friday night Takako, Lisa and he watch a video together or play a board game. His daughter Lisa recently made her first shopping trip to the mall with a girlfriend. She purchased a micro skirt that she wants to wear to a school social this upcoming Friday. The skirt does not meet the school dress code.

The author would like to close this note by recognizing his kids, step-kids and spouses, current and former: Lisa, James, Pat, Will, Brook, Margaret, Chico, Takako, and Morgan. They, as much as art, have made life worthwhile.